My first book of
NEW YORK

Ingela P. Arrhenius

WALKER BOOKS

BROOKLYN

Thousands of cars, bikes, and people cross the bridge between Manhattan and Brooklyn every day. More people live in Brooklyn than in any of the other four New York boroughs. It has great shops and even a famous amusement park.

Brooklyn Bridge

East River

Brooklyn Academy
of Music

pizza

dog walker

brownstone
building

flea market

NEW YORK WATER TAXI

water taxi

Ice

TICKETS   Snacks   Pizza   Ice Cream

Italian ice

Coney Island

ROCKEFELLER CENTER

At Christmas this is a magical place to be. You can ice skate beneath the huge Christmas tree or catch a spectacular show at Radio City Music Hall.

Rockefeller Center

Top of the Rock observation deck

The Rockettes

Radio City Music Hall

cheesecake

St. Patrick's Cathedral

pastrami on rye

Museum of Modern Art

CHINATOWN

New York is full of vibrant neighborhoods created by immigrants from all over the world. Chinatown and Little Italy are both famous for their restaurants and markets.

tourist

deli

Soups

Fresh

market

dim sum

Tenement Museum

cannoli

Little Italy

mah-jongg players

EMPIRE STATE BUILDING

For amazing views over the city, take the elevator up to the top of this Midtown skyscraper. You'll be able to see the crowds headed to Madison Square Garden.

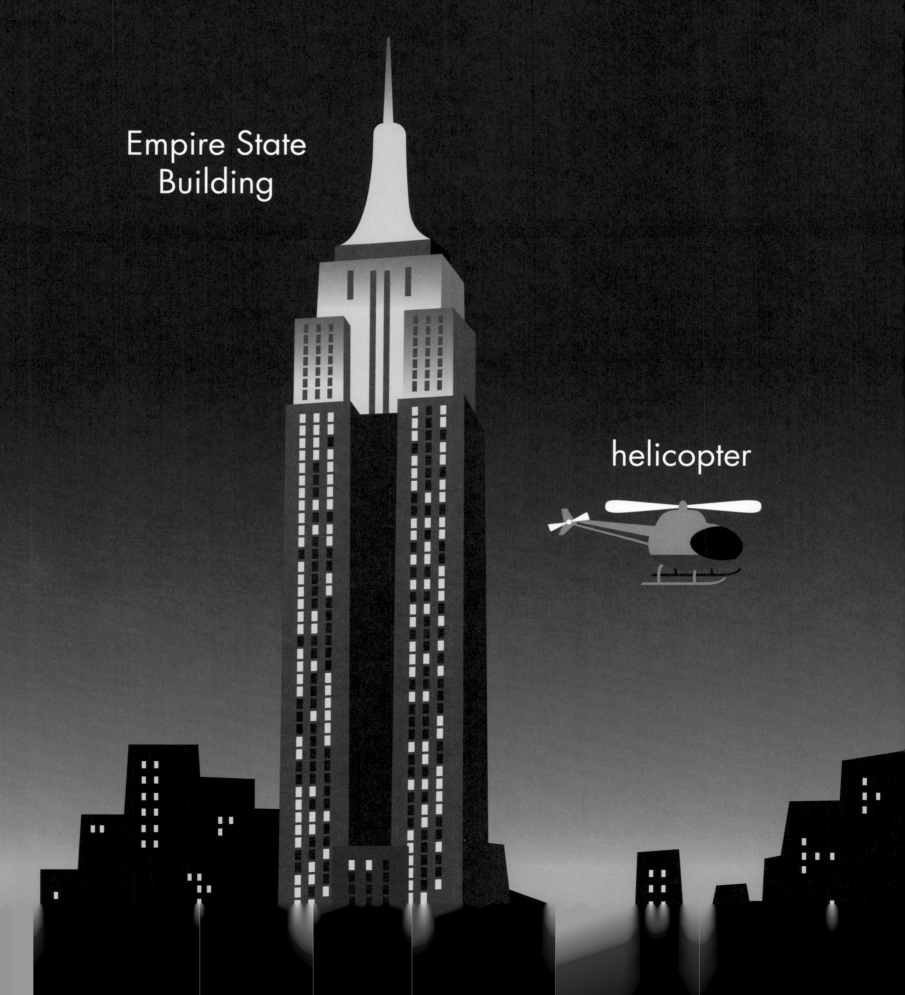

Empire State
Building

helicopter

ice hockey player

basketball player

peregrine falcon

Flatiron Building

bibimbap

Koreatown

elevator

coffee

Madison Square Garden

GREENWICH VILLAGE

Artists and performers have always loved the lively streets of the Village. Walk the High Line, a park built on an old train line above the city, and you'll find your way to the cafés, galleries, and markets of nearby Chelsea.

Washington Square Park

Chelsea Market

The Stonewall Inn

coffee shop

High Line

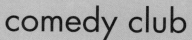

comedy club

fire truck

Children's Museum of the Arts

Grand Central Terminal

It's always busy at this station. Thousands of people rush through to catch trains every day. For some peace and quiet, the New York Public Library is nearby.

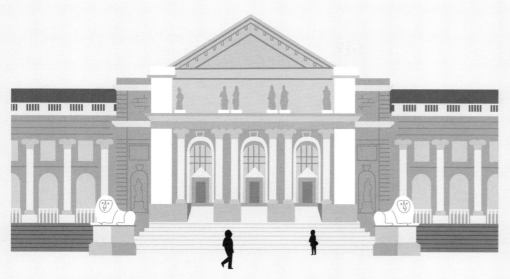

New York Public Library

subway

Chrysler Building

Bryant Park

oyster bar

DIAMONDS
WE BUY DIAMONDS
OPEN 7 DAYS

Diamond District

United Nations headquarters

HARLEM

This bustling neighborhood is a great place to listen to some jazz music, catch a show at the historic Apollo Theater, or enjoy an exhibition at El Museo del Barrio. Or, head to nearby Washington Heights to visit the Cloisters, a museum built from elements of medieval French abbeys.

Apollo Theater

The Cloisters

jazz club

fire hydrant

mural

soul food

El Museo del Barrio

tour guide

mailbox

MUSEUMS

New York is famous for its many museums and galleries where you can see art and artifacts from all over the world. There's natural history on display too — look out for the whale!

Metropolitan Museum of Art

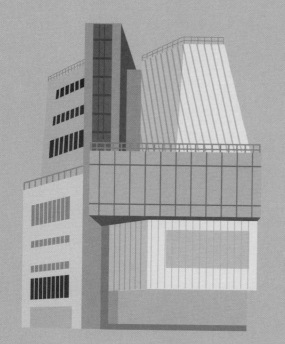

Whitney Museum
of American Art

American Museum
of Natural History

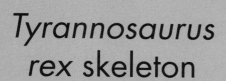

modern art

blue whale model

sculpture

Tyrannosaurus
rex skeleton

Solomon R.
Guggenheim
Museum

Queens

There are lots of different sports to experience in the city's largest borough, from horse racing to tennis. You can also watch the New York Mets baseball team.

Flushing Meadows Corona Park

airplane

Jamaica Bay Wildlife Refuge

tennis
player

Belmont Park racecourse

falafel

marathon
runners

Little India

RESTAURANT

Greek restaurant

Mexican
restaurant

Central Park

Right in the middle of Manhattan, this park is always full of joggers, cyclists, and visitors. Explore woods and lakes, ride the carousel, or visit the zoo.

Bow Bridge

carousel

model boats

Belvedere Castle

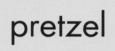

pretzel

zoo

Alice in Wonderland statue

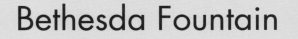

jogger

Bethesda Fountain

Strawberry Fields

SHOPPING

From small fashion boutiques to grand department stores, New York has shops to suit everyone.

car

Fifth Avenue

shoppers

Tiffany & Co.

Macy's Thanksgiving Day Parade

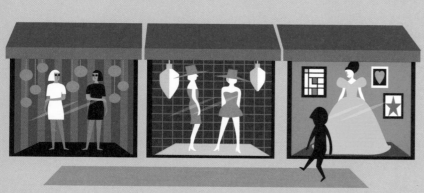

Saks Fifth Avenue
window display

FAO Schwarz

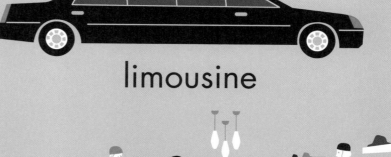

limousine

Union Square Greenmarket

SoHo fashion shop

STATUE OF LIBERTY

This symbol of New York, its most famous monument, stands in the harbor of the city. You can reach it by ferry and also visit Ellis Island, where immigrants arriving in America used to be registered.

Statue of Liberty

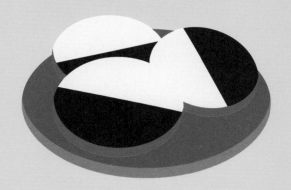

black-and-white cookies

National Museum of the American Indian

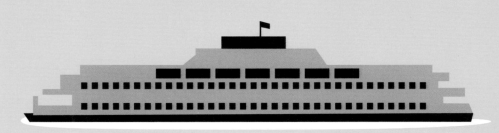

Staten Island Ferry

Ellis Island

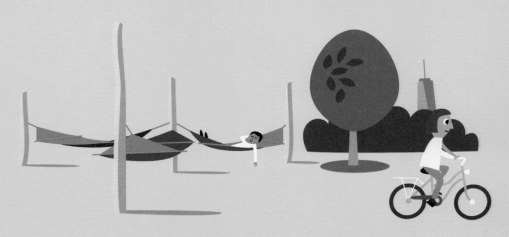

passport

bagel

Governors Island

THE BRONX

This neighborhood in the north of New York is home to the world-famous Yankees baseball team. There's plenty to see as well at the zoo and botanical garden.

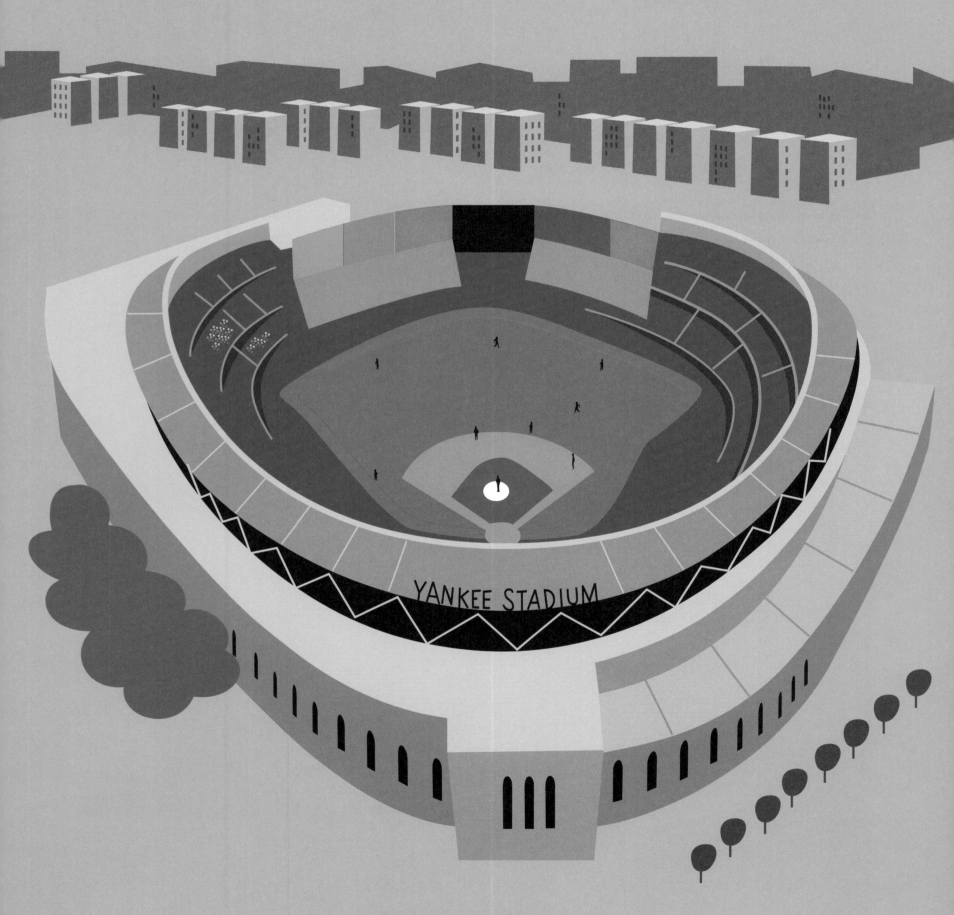

YANKEE STADIUM

Yankee Stadium

hot dog

soda

doughnuts

street dancer

New York Botanical Garden

baseball player

bus

Bronx Zoo

water tank

WALL STREET

This is the heart of the city's Financial District. Its many skyscrapers are filled with busy office workers.

New York
Stock
Exchange

Fearless Girl statue

sushi

One World
Trade Center

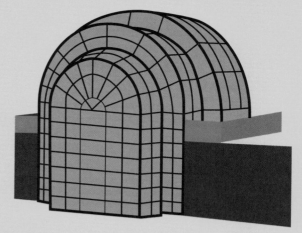

Winter Garden Atrium

Woolworth
Building

The Battery

*Charging
Bull* statue

office workers

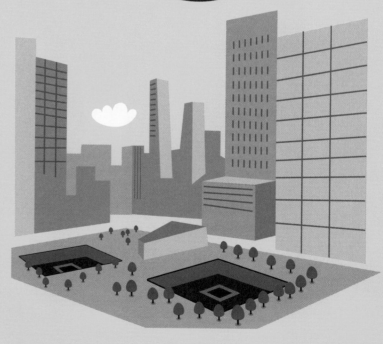

National September 11
Memorial & Museum

Times Square & Broadway

*Be dazzled by the bright lights of Times Square!
There are lots of theaters on Broadway if you want to catch a
show. Or you could watch one of the street performers who
entertain the crowds here.*

Times
Square

THE PLAY

A

NEW

HEY

BROADWAY

yellow taxi

Lincoln Center

hot-dog cart

street
performer

candy

tickets

theaters

police officer

To my mom and dad,
who took me to New York when I was twelve.

What I remember the most from that trip as a child are the big cars, the skyscrapers, the melted-cheese sandwiches, the skaters at Rockefeller Center . . . and that I bought myself an Olivia Newton-John record! I hope this book will remind others of New York memories.

Copyright © 2019 by Ingela P. Arrhenius

First U.S. edition 2019

Library of Congress Catalog Card Number 2019939002
ISBN 978-1-5362-0990-7

24 CCP 10 9 8 7 6 5

Printed in Shenzhen, Guangdong, China

This book was typeset in Futura.
The illustrations were created digitally.

Walker Books U.S.
a division of
Candlewick Press
99 Dover Street
Somerville, Massachusetts 02144

www.walkerbooksus.com